This book belongs to

....

....

Copyright © Angus Hudson Ltd/Three's
Company 1996

Text and illustrations by Eira B. Reeves

First published in the UK by Candle Books

ISBN 1 85985 136 3

Distributed by SP Trust
Triangle Business Park
Wendover Road
Stoke Mandeville
Aylesbury
Bucks. England

Designed by Peter Wyart at Three's
Company

Worldwide coedition organised and
produced by
Angus Hudson Ltd,
Concorde House, Grenville Place,
Mill Hill, London NW7 3SA, England
Tel: +44 181 959 3668
Fax: +44 181 959 3678

Printed in Singapore

MY FIRST PICTURE BIBLE
Eira Reeves

CONTENTS

Abraham leaves home

Long, long ago, in a far-off land called Ur, there lived a man named Abram.

One day God spoke to him.
'I am going to give you a special land,' God promised.
'Look up! Can you count the stars?
One day there will be more people in your family
than stars in the sky!'

So Abram packed his bags
and loaded up his animals.
Then he set out with his family
to look for this special land.
He believed God.

After travelling for many months,
Abram came at last to the land God promised.
There he stayed with his wife, Sarah,
and their son, Isaac.

Genesis 12:1–9, 21:1–7

11

God changed Abram's name to Abraham.
God blessed Abraham with great flocks of sheep
and herds of camels.

Now Abraham's son, Isaac, had two sons,
Esau and Jacob.
Esau was a hunter.
But Jacob, the younger son,
was very crafty.

One day Jacob went to his blind, old father
and pretended that he was Esau.
So Isaac gave Jacob his special blessing
instead of Esau.

Esau was so angry that Jacob had to run away.
He went to a far country.

Genesis 25:19–34, 27:1–45

One night, as he slept on a rock,
Jacob dreamed he saw angels
climbing up and down a ladder to heaven.
'I will always look after your family,'
God promised.

Genesis 28:10–22

Years later Jacob came back to the Promised Land
and made it up with his brother Esau.
By now Jacob had a big family of twelve sons.

But Jacob's young son, Joseph, was his favourite.
Jacob gave him a richly coloured coat.
How smart he looked!

. . . And how jealous his brothers were!
They were so angry that one day they took
Joseph and sold him to traders going to Egypt.
They told their father Jacob
that Joseph had been killed.
He wept.

Genesis 37:1–36

19

One year no rain fell.
No one could find enough food to eat.
But in Egypt, Joseph had saved grain
in great storehouses.

Genesis 38–41

Joseph had lots of adventures in Egypt.
First he was slave to an army captain,
then he was thrown into prison,
and finally he was made chief minister
of Pharaoh, the king of Egypt!

When Jacob heard this, he took his family to
Egypt to get food.
How glad he was to find his son Joseph alive!

Genesis 42–47

Moses leads his
people out of Egypt

So Joseph's family settled in Egypt. They were called Hebrews.
The family grew bigger and bigger!
Years later a new Pharaoh ruled, who had never known Joseph.
He made the Hebrews work as slaves.

Exodus 1

Pharaoh was scared that
there were so many
Hebrews.
'Kill every Hebrew baby
boy,' he ordered.

But one Hebrew mother hid her
baby, Moses, in a basket.
Pharaoh's own daughter, the
princess of Egypt, found the
basket floating in the river.
Moses was saved.

Exodus 2:1–11

So the princess took baby Moses to the palace.
He was brought up as a royal prince.

When Moses grew up, he ran away from
Egypt and lived in the desert.
One day an angel from God spoke to Moses
from a burning bush:
'Go and tell Pharaoh: "Let my people go!"'

Exodus 3

Moses was scared.
But he went to Pharaoh
many times, saying
'Let my people go!'
At last Pharaoh gave in.
'Go – and take all your
people with you!'

Exodus 10:21–29

The Hebrews got ready hastily to leave.
Then they set out for the land
that God had promised them.

Exodus 12

Pharaoh chased after the Hebrews. But when he came to the Red Sea, he and all his soldiers were drowned. God had saved his people again!

Exodus 14

The Hebrews stayed in the desert for many years.
God gave them special food called manna.
Often they grumbled and moaned.
They even worshipped a gold statue instead of God.

Exodus 16, 32

One day Moses climbed a very high mountain. When he came down he carried two great stones. On them were written God's special rules for everyone. We call these the Ten Commandments.

Exodus 20

God told his people to build a special big tent,
where priests could pray to God.
When they moved on, they could fold up the tent
and carry it with them.

Exodus 26

Into the Promised Land

As they got closer to the Promised Land,
Moses sent spies to explore.
Two came back and said
'It is a land full of fruits and good food!'

Numbers 13

At last, after Moses died,
God's people crossed the river Jordan.
They entered the Promised Land.
But still they had to capture the land.

Joshua 3–4

37

God gave special orders for attacking the city of Jericho.
The people walked round and round it.
When the trumpets blew, the people shouted and the walls fell in!

Joshua 5:13–6:27

Now God gave his people special new leaders.
One great leader was named Gideon.

Judges 6

With God's help, Gideon beat the Israelites' enemies.
He attacked by night, scaring them with flaming torches and
lots of noise! They ran away terrified.

Judges 7

At harvest time, the people had a great festival.
They thanked God for all the fruits and grain in the promised land.

Leviticus 23

But the people were not happy. 'Give us a king!' they demanded.
'Everyone else has a king.'

1 Samuel 8

42

Kings and Prophets

So God told his prophet Samuel
where to find a man fit to be
king of Israel.
His name was Saul.

Samuel poured oil on Saul's head.
This showed that he had been chosen
by God to be king.

1 Samuel 9–10

At first King Saul ruled well.
He led his armies against many enemies.

1 Samuel 14:15–23

46

But later Saul disobeyed God.
So God sent Samuel to find a new king.

1 Samuel 15

He found a boy looking after his father's sheep in the fields.
His name was David.
Samuel knew that he had been chosen
by God to be the next king.

1 Samuel 16

David was brave.
He fought the giant Goliath
with his shepherd's sling and killed him.
The people sang 'How brave he is!'

1 Samuel 17

King David was a great ruler.
He loved to play his harp and sing of God's love.

He made the beautiful city of Jerusalem his capital.

2 Samuel 5

David brought the special box containing
the Ten Commandments to Jerusalem.
He danced and sang in front of it.

2 Samuel 6

When David died, his son Solomon became king.
Solomon was very wise.

1 Kings 2

53

When the people had problems,
they came to him to ask what they should do.

1 Kings 3

The Queen of Sheba, who lived far, far away, travelled for days to hear Solomon's wise words.

1 Kings 10:1–14

King Solomon built a beautiful
new temple in Jerusalem.
It was made of the best gold,
wood and stone.

1 Kings 6

The people disobey God

But after Solomon died, the people disobeyed many of God's laws.
The kingdom split into two;
one part was called Judah and the other Israel.

God sent special messangers, called prophets,
to tell the people to return to God's way.
The prophet Elijah warned wicked king Ahab.

'Worship the living God,' Elijah said.
When he prayed, God sent down fire from heaven.

1 Kings 17–18

60

God sent many other prophets.
Jeremiah warned that there would be war
if the people did not turn to God.

God sent other prophets:
Isaiah, Daniel, Jonah
and a shepherd prophet,
named Amos.

They warned the Israelites,
'Mend your ways,
or God will send enemies
to defeat you.'

But still they didn't listen.
So cruel kings came from Assyria and
Babylon and took the Israelites away
to be slaves. They destroyed the
beautiful city of Jerusalem.

2 Kings 25

64

But the prophets also had a message of hope.
'God still loves you,' they said.
'He is going to send a very special person,' they promised.
'He will save us.'

So many years later, that special person came, just as God promised. His name was **_Jesus._**

The story of Jesus

Many, many years ago, Jewish prophets foretold that a special Man would be born in the town of Bethlehem.

Isaiah 7:14

They said He would be
called the Prince of Peace.

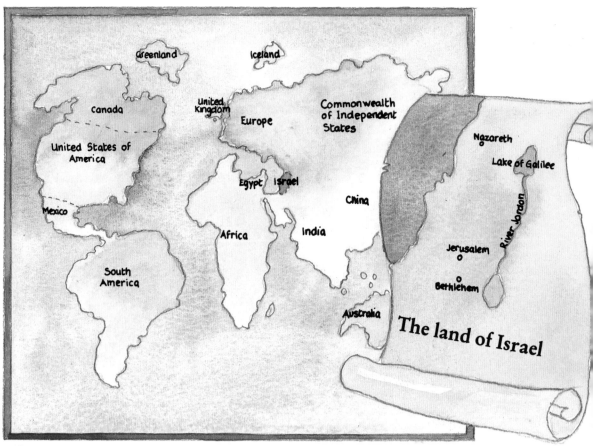

The World

The first Christmas

It all began in a little town called
Nazareth...

In Nazareth there lived a young
woman called Mary.
One day an angel appeared to her.
He said, 'You will give birth to a
very special baby. You must call
the baby Jesus.'

Luke 1:26–38

73

Mary went quickly to tell her cousin Elizabeth the good news.
Elizabeth was expecting a baby too.
His name was to be John.
Both women were overjoyed.

Mary was married to a carpenter named Joseph.
They had to go on a long journey to Bethlehem.
Mary was very tired when they arrived.

Luke 2:1–7

At first they could find nowhere to sleep.

Then a hotel-keeper found them a stable, where the animals were kept. Mary and Joseph took it gladly.

That night some shepherds were sleeping in a field near
Bethlehem. Suddenly they saw a bright light. An angel
appeared and said, 'Tonight a child has been born in
Bethlehem. He has come to save His people.'

78

Immediately the shepherds set off to find the newborn baby.

Luke 2:8–20

Far away, some wise men saw a special new star in the sky. They knew they must follow this star to find a special baby. So they brought gifts of gold, frankincense and myrrh to give to the child.

The visitors came to the little town of Bethlehem, where the star was shining down.

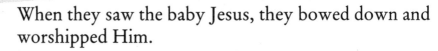

When they saw the baby Jesus, they bowed down and worshipped Him.

Matthew 2:1–12

Jesus
grows up

Mary and Joseph took Jesus back to their own town, Nazareth.

Here Jesus grew up. He helped His parents
and played with His friends.

Matthew 2:19–23

When Jesus was twelve, He went with His parents to the city
of Jerusalem for the festival called Passover.
But Mary and Joseph lost Him in the crowd.

At last they found their son again; He was talking to the Jewish teachers in the Temple.
Everyone was amazed at the wise things He said.

Luke 2:41–52

As the years passed, Jesus grew up.
He began to work as a carpenter,
like His father Joseph.
He was happy working with His
hammer and saw.
But He knew that God had a very
special job for Him to do.

Jesus' special work

At this time Jesus' cousin, John, started to preach
by the river Jordan.
He told people to turn from the bad things they were doing.

He dipped them in the river to
show that they were making a
clean start.

Jesus came to the river and asked John to baptize Him too.

The Holy Spirit came down on
Him like a dove.

Luke 3:1–22

This was the beginning of Jesus'
special work, the work God
wanted Him to do.

Luke 3:1–22

Now Jesus went to the lake. He called twelve men to be His special followers. These men were called disciples.

Their names are:
Simon Peter
and his brother
Andrew,
James
and his brother *John,*
Philip,
Bartholomew,
Matthew the tax-man,
Thomas the twin,
another *James,*
Simon,
Judas, James' son,
and *Judas.*

Mark 1:14–20, 3:13–19

He taught His disciples
how to pray to God, our
heavenly Father:

Our Father in heaven:
Holy is Your name;
May Your kingdom
    come;
May Your will be done
on earth as it is in heaven.
Give us today the food we
    need.
Forgive us the wrong we
    have done,
as we forgive those who
    have wronged us.
Do not bring us to hard
    testing,
but keep us safe from evil.
    Amen.

Matthew 6:9–15

Jesus began to travel to nearby towns and villages.

He told people special stories about how God wants our world to be. Everyone was amazed when they heard Him speak.

Jesus loved children.
He said that we should love them and take good care of them.

He wanted all people to love
one another.
He told us always to forgive
each other.

Many sick people came to Jesus – people who were crippled, blind or deaf.

Jesus healed them.

And with His Father's help Jesus did special miracles.
One day He fed five thousand people with just five loaves and
two fish!

Luke 9:10–17

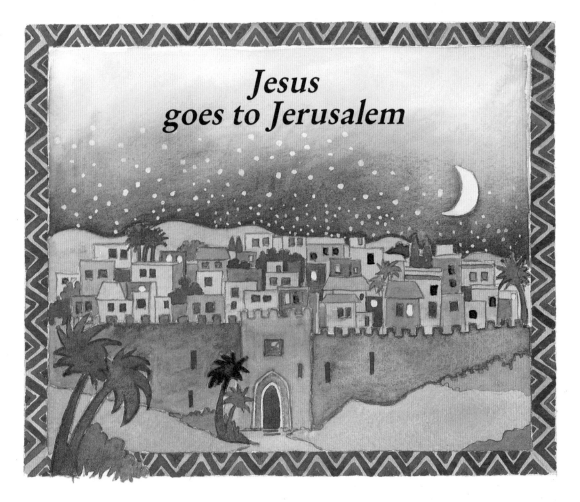

Jesus
goes to Jerusalem

Jesus loved Jerusalem, the capital city.
It was very beautiful.

Jesus decided to travel to Jerusalem again.
On the way, He said to His disciples, 'I am going to die soon.'
The disciples were sad. They didn't know why He was
saying such things.

But some of the leaders in Jerusalem hated Jesus.
They thought He wasn't keeping their laws.
So they plotted to kill Him.

Judas, one of the disciples, turned against Jesus.
He made a secret plan with the people who hated Jesus.

Luke 22:1–6

When Jesus arrived in Jerusalem it was the time of the
Passover festival again. He asked to borrow a donkey,
because He wanted to ride into the city.

When they saw Him coming, people waved palm leaves.
'Jesus is our King!' they shouted.

Later, Jesus had a special feast with His disciples.
He said once more, 'I am going to die soon!'
But they didn't understand why He was saying this.

Jesus tore off some bread and poured some wine. He said,
'Each time you eat bread and drink wine, remember Me.'

Luke 22:7–23

Then Jesus and the disciples went out into a garden.
Jesus prayed to His heavenly Father.
But the disciples fell asleep.

Luke 22:39–46

The
first Easter

While they were in the garden, Judas brought Jesus' enemies
to arrest Him.
Jesus' disciples and friends all ran away.

The soldiers brought Jesus before the Roman ruler, Pilate.
But Pilate could find no fault in Jesus.

When Pilate brought Jesus before
the people, they shouted,
'Kill Him! Kill Him!'

Luke 22:47–53, 22:66–23:25

The soldiers took Jesus and put Him to death
on a wooden cross.

Luke 23:26–46

119

Jesus' friends and
family were very sad.
They had lost a very
special friend and
leader.

They took Jesus' body, wrapped it carefully in cloth, and laid it in a cave tomb.
A great round stone was rolled across the door.

Luke 23:50–56

Two days later Peter and John,
Jesus' disciples, went to visit the tomb.
But the stone had been rolled away.
They were amazed!

John 20:1–9

122

They saw an angel inside the tomb.
He said, 'Don't be afraid! Jesus is alive!
Go and meet Him in Galilee.'

Soon afterwards the disciples went fishing on the lake of Galilee.

They saw Jesus on the beach, making a fire. He invited them to have breakfast.

Peter was so pleased to see Jesus that he jumped into the water and waded ashore.

John 21:1–14

In Jerusalem, soon after this, Jesus left them.
He returned to His heavenly Father.
Now the disciples knew He was alive forever.

And Jesus promised to return one day as King ...